On Set

Written by
Daisy Hawkins

Illustrated by
Pablo Gallego

Published in 2026 by
Norwood House Press
2544 Clinton Street
Buffalo, NY 14224

Printed in the United States of America

Library of Congress Cataloging-in-Publication Data:
Names: Hawkins, Daisy, author. | Gallego, Pablo, illustrator.
Title: On set / written by Daisy Hawkins, illustrated by Pablo Gallego. In the gap / written by Daisy Hawkins.
Description: Buffalo, NY : Norwood House Press, 2026. | Series: Phonics all-stars: phase 2 |
Identifiers: ISBN 9781978577787 (pbk.) | ISBN 9781978577794 (library bound) | ISBN 9781978577800 (ebook)
Subjects: LCSH: Reading–Phonetic method–Juvenile literature. | English language–Phonetics–Juvenile literature. | Contests–Juvenile literature. | Television–Juvenile literature. | Caves–Juvenile literature.
Classification: LCC LB1573.3 H395 2026 | DDC 372.465–dc23

CPSIA compliance information: Batch #CW26NHP: For further information contact Norwood House Press at 1-800-237-9932.

Bill is on set.

Tess is on set.

3 ... 2 ... 1 ... Go!

Tess passes Bill on logs.

Bill is not hot
on the log run.

Tess tucks up to fit in the gap.

Can Bill?

Tess ducks and
can miss the mud.

Bill did not duck.
Bill fell in the mud.

Can Tess get to the top of the big red hill?

Can Bill?

Bill and Tess on set.

In the Gap

By Daisy Hawkins

Can Lil go in the gap in the hill?

Lil can go in the gap,
but the sun can not.

In the gap,
moss sits on the rock.

In the gap,
bugs hum and hiss.

In the gap,
bats fill the back.

In the gap,
Lil is not in luck.

Lil can not miss the bats.

In the gap,
a bat is the boss.